18ᵀᴴ CENTURY PAPERCUTTING

How Richard Hall illustrated his world.

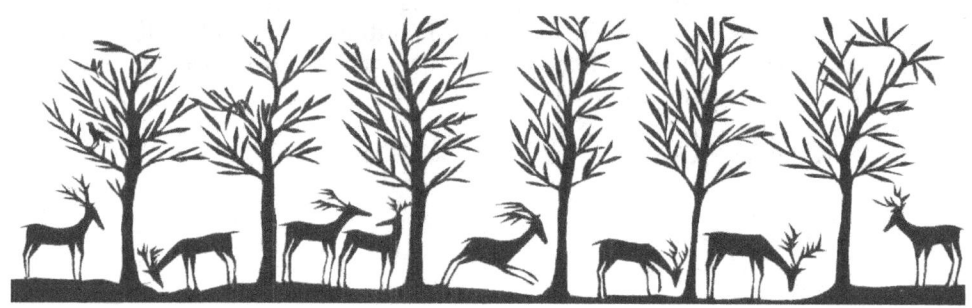

Illustrations crafted by Richard Hall
and text by his descendant Mike Rendell

ISBN-13: 978-1479262304

ISBN-10: 1479262307

To Philippa: to whom I owe everything.

Introduction

Richard Hall was my great-great-great-great grandfather, living between 1729 and 1801. He was a hosier with a shop at Number One London Bridge. Later, after his first wife died, he fell out with his children (they disapproved of his choice of second wife) and went to live in Bourton-on-the-Water in the Cotswolds, where he raised a second family.

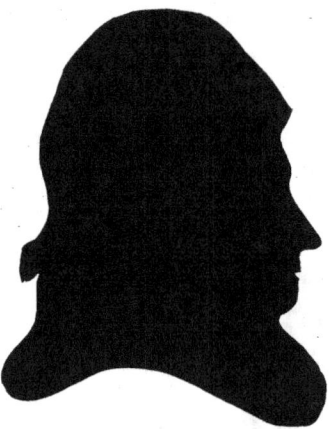

A silhouette of Richard Hall, probably taken by his daughter Martha. (Note: silhouettes, like photographs, are described as being 'taken' rather than 'made').

Richard must have had excellent eyesight, a steady hand, and an artistic talent, no doubt linked to his training as an embroiderer and maker of silk stockings. Using small, sharp, scissors and a pen knife (literally a knife for cutting quill feathers with which to make pens) he cut out dozens of pictures of country scenes – probably to amuse his young family. Many of the cut-outs depict travel, farming and every-day life and in all probability were made in the last twenty years of Richard's life (in other words between 1780 and 1800). Some of the cut-outs are incredibly finely made – with horses' reins hardly wider than a human hair - and it is remarkable that they have survived two centuries virtually intact.

Because they were not framed or protected, they were simply kept between the pages of a couple of notebooks. In turn these were placed in a horse-hair chest after Richard died, along with a huge array of his personal papers, journals etc. Over the course of the next 200 years the chest languished unopened, along with a whole array of Richard's belongings – his books, his fossil and shell collections, his silver cutlery and above all, his diaries. The collection of memorabilia stayed intact whenever the family moved, and came into my possession when I bought my grand-mothers house in the 1970's. She had lived in the same place for over 50 years – and eventually I got around to opening the old trunk and numerous battered tea chests. The papers inside formed the basis for my research into the life of Richard.

In 2011 I published Richard's story as a social history of England in the Eighteenth Century – the world seen through his eyes. Entitled *The Journal of a Georgian Gentleman* I illustrated it with some of Richard's cut-outs. After it was published I realized that some of the cut-outs might appeal to modern-day proponents of the craft, and googled "paper cutters." I was astonished to see how popular this craft was, especially in the United States where the German tradition of *scheren schnitte* (literally 'scissor cut') has firmly taken root. There is a Guild of American Paper Cutters, even a small museum (in the town of Somerset, Pennsylvania) and regular journals.

The tools and techniques.

Only two of the paper cuts are dated (1780 and 1798) but there is every indication that this spread of nearly twenty years covers the majority of the cut-outs. By that time Richard was retired, and would have had time to make the pictures using natural daylight. (I simply cannot imagine him being able to carry out such fine scissor-work by a flickering candlelight!).

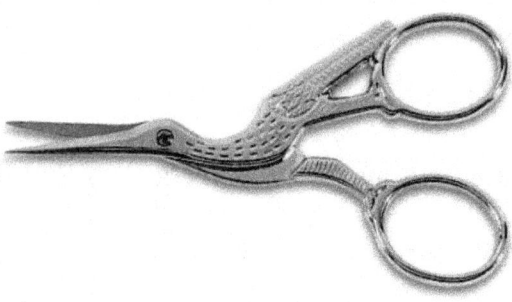

Richard would have used a pair of steel scissors not dissimilar to these modern Gingher scissors – very sharp, with a blade less than one and a half inches long. The entire pair of scissors is just three and a half inches long.

Richard also owned this knife, which has fortunately survived intact in its specially-made case.

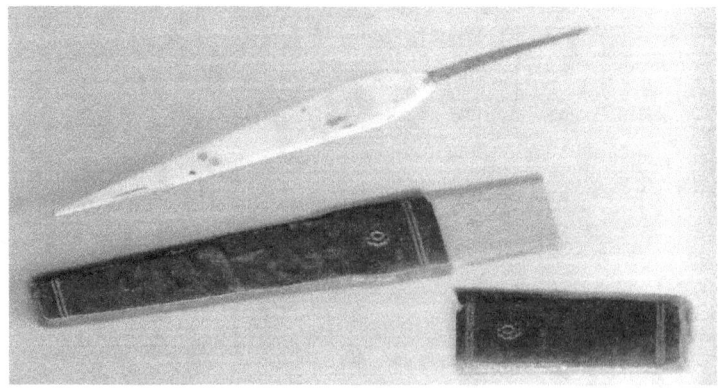

The paper which Richard used was white and hand-made. It was largely free from the acid used in modern paper manufacture. Why white? Because in the eighteenth century smooth black paper was hard to come by – the blackening process left the paper as course as fine sand-paper and hence unable to take the sharp edge which was needed in a cut-out.

Richard kept the cut-outs in between the leaves of an ordinary note book, with tissue paper separating the illustrations where two or more pieces were stored together.

A clue as to how Richard made the cut-outs appears in this unfinished version of what would have been a horse and carriage scene. The top half was worked on first, removing paper to show the outlines, before more detailed work was carried out to each separate part of the design. The lower strip was kept intact – over half an inch wide to allow for easy handling. The final part of the process would be to cut off this foreground to leave a fragile and delicate picture.

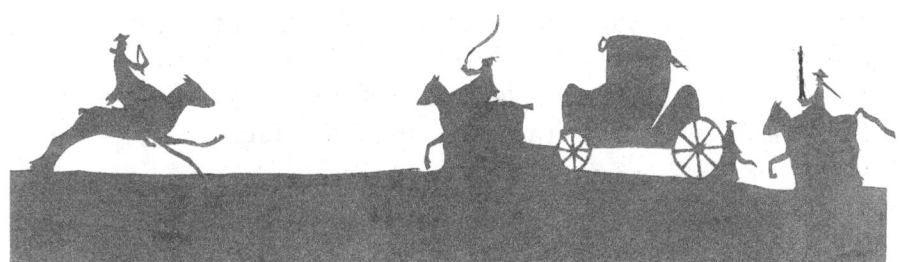

The Paper cuts

Because Richard used white paper for cutting out it makes sense to print the images in negative form to contrast with the white background of this book. Changing the image to negative does give a very different feel to the cut-outs – here as an example is a picture of a coach-and-four in its original white-on-black form, shown flipped to face right, and a negative image i.e. black on white, shown as I suspect it was cut, i.e. facing left.

The detail is astonishing – as in the traces linking the horses together. The picture appears to show leaf springs over the wheels, but these are insufficient to stop the heads of the two passengers bobbing up and down so that the tails of their wigs fly up in the air! Richard has even decorated the side panel of the coach with what appear to be stars and crescent moons. Incidentally the whip held by the rider at the front has got folded over – it should be straight – a reminder of how delicate these cut-outs are, and how being clamped tight between other pages for two centuries has not always given protection.

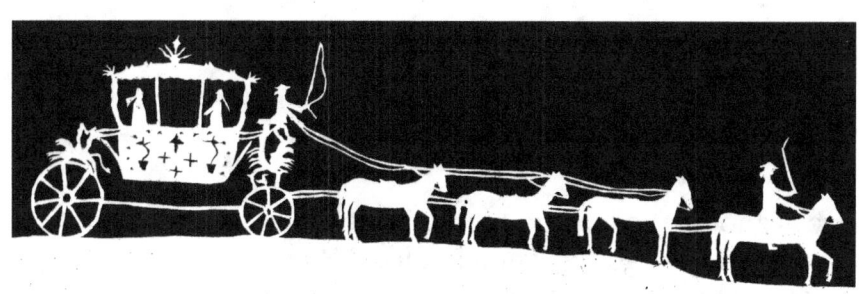

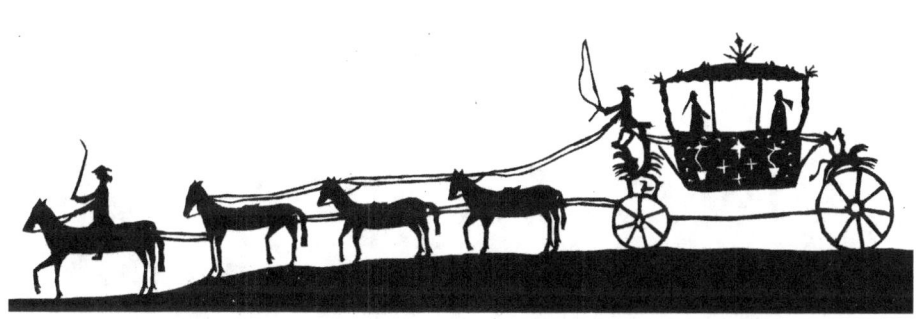

Here is another coach and four, with the front wheel about to crash down after going over a boulder! Richard would have been well aware of the discomfort of travelling long distances on poor roads – carriage springs only came in late in the century, and roads were in a very rough state until the turnpike trusts led to significant improvements.

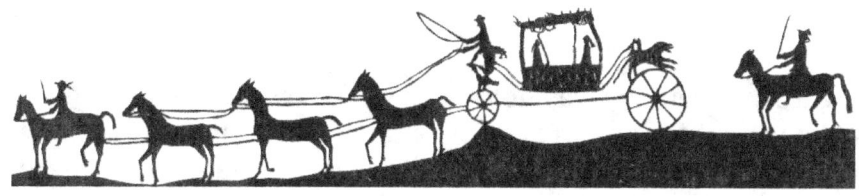

The eighteenth century was notorious for highwaymen, who would lie in wait for passing travellers and accost them in some suitably deserted spot with the cry of "Stand and deliver." Richard illustrates the scene with the robber holding up a coach with his blunderbuss in one hand, and his sword in the other. The dog appears to draw back, as if barking at the robber.

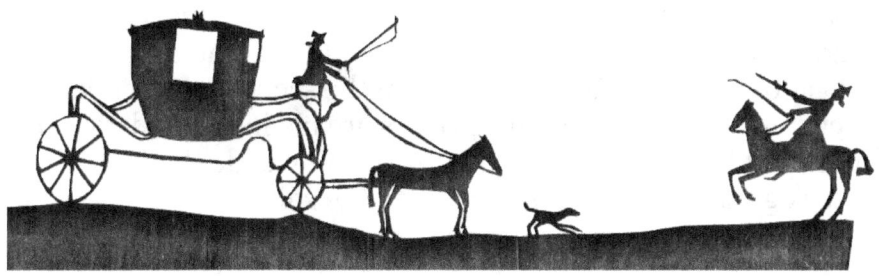

Capital punishment was a feature of 'Justice' in the 1700's and anyone convicted of highway robbery would find themselves sent to the gallows. This is Richard's take on the scene – so mundane an occurrence that the two horse riders are having a good gossip, seemingly oblivious to the macabre scene alongside them. Livestock graze and lock horns beneath the gallows....

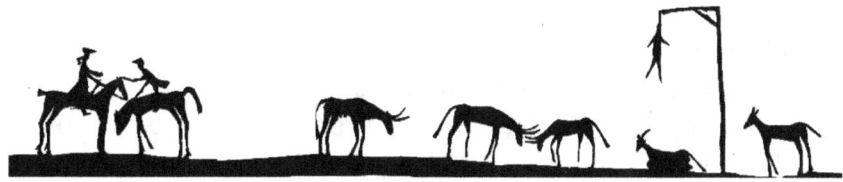

Where Richard lived in London, right by London Bridge, he was close to the main coaching inns where the horses were kept and where coaches would collect and drop off passengers. Here is one showing the word 'Lyn' on the coach door – perhaps an indication that it was the King's Lynn coach from Norfolk. Passengers sit 'up top' as the coach draws in to the stop, where an ostler prepares to assist a rider dismount. The inn sign is indecipherable but may perhaps be The Three Tuns.

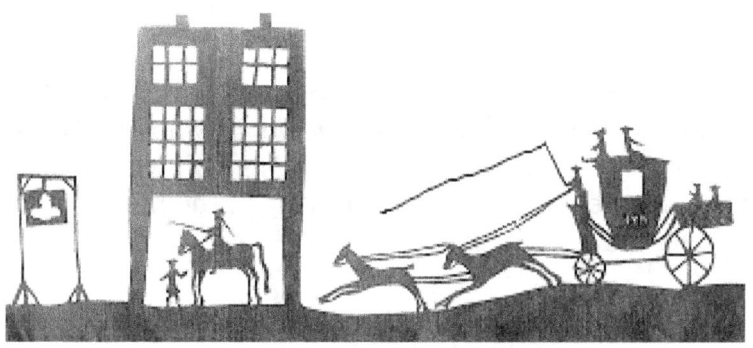

Twice a year, Richard would leave London and head for the Cotswolds, where he owned Bengeworth Mansion House near Evesham. (It is now the Evesham Hotel, shown below). Richard shows the scene of a carriage arriving at the house while, on the left, deer gambol around.

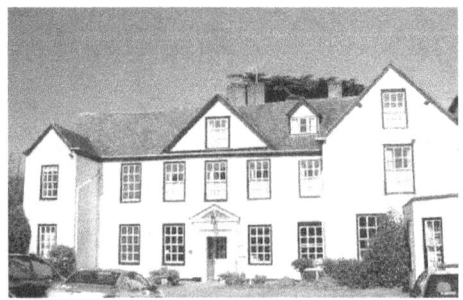

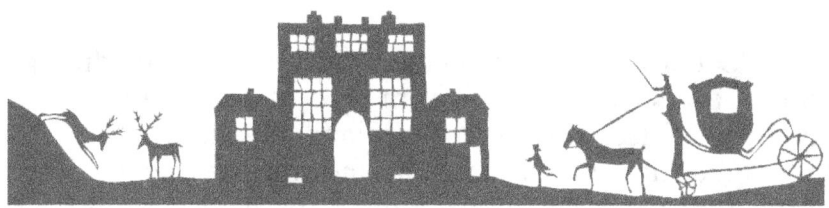

While in the Cotswolds Richard made a diary entry about 'dining on a haunch of venison' - perhaps from his own deer. Here is a delightful scene of deer grazing in woodland. The differences in the stance of the animals is fascinating, showing the way the deer inter-relate. A blackbird sits in the branches of the tree on the left....

In the lower picture Richard observes a herd of deer– a youngster is suckling its mother, two others lock horns, while others stand and watch.

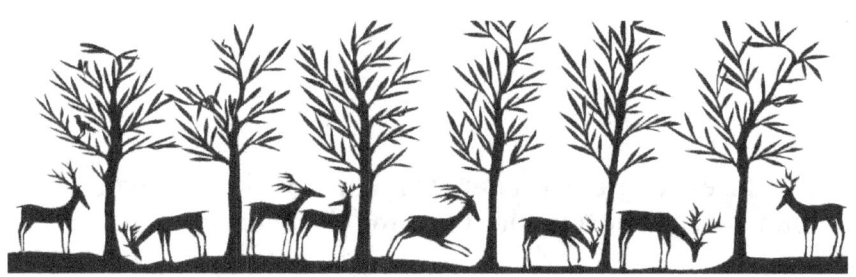

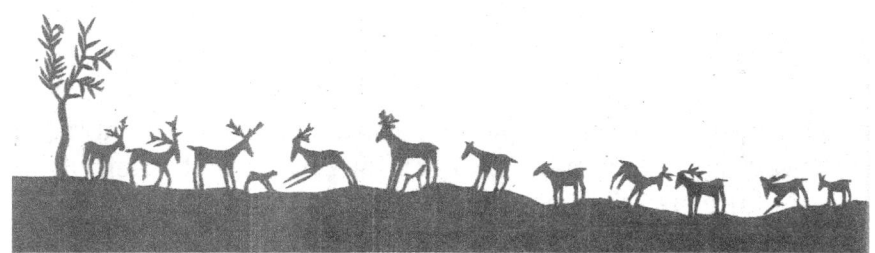

Richard's diaries refer to the cherry orchards which he owned. Here a man is climbing a ladder to prune the cherry trees - somewhat precariously – while a second man sweeps up the clippings.

In the lower picture a farmer ploughs the land behind two horses under the guidance of a man holding a long whip. To the left of the gate a figure seeks to keep control of a bounding dog.

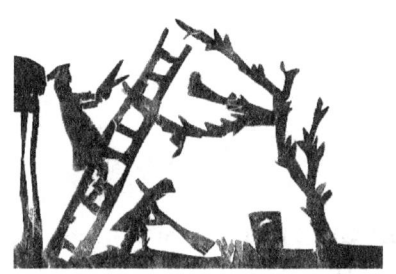

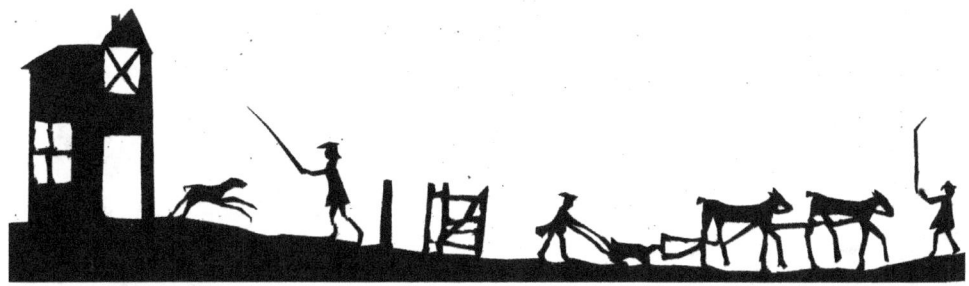

Living in the country meant rural pursuits – point-to-point racing, and even fox hunting.

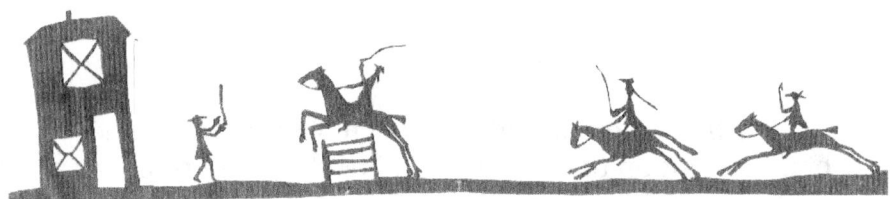

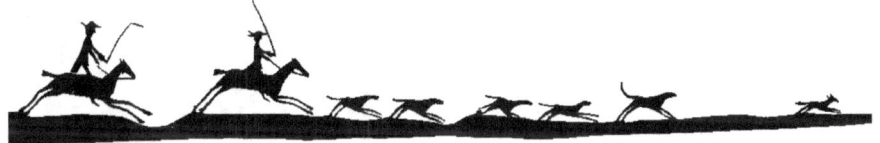

In the winter fresh meat would have been obtained from the dovecote. Birds sit on the dovecote and feed on the ground as a man approaches. The figure on the left is possibly digging the soil with a spade.

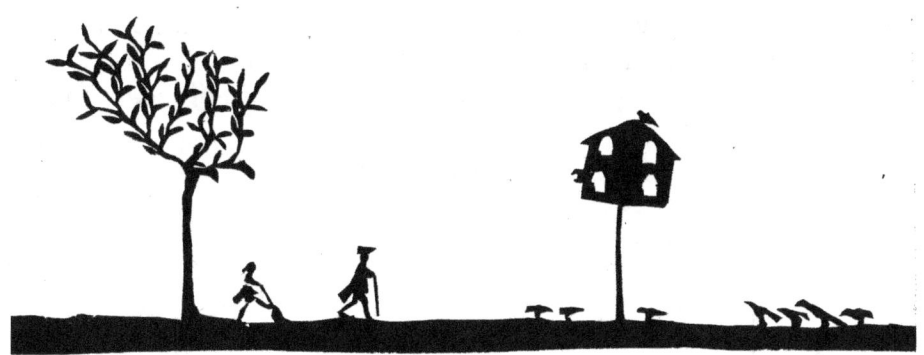

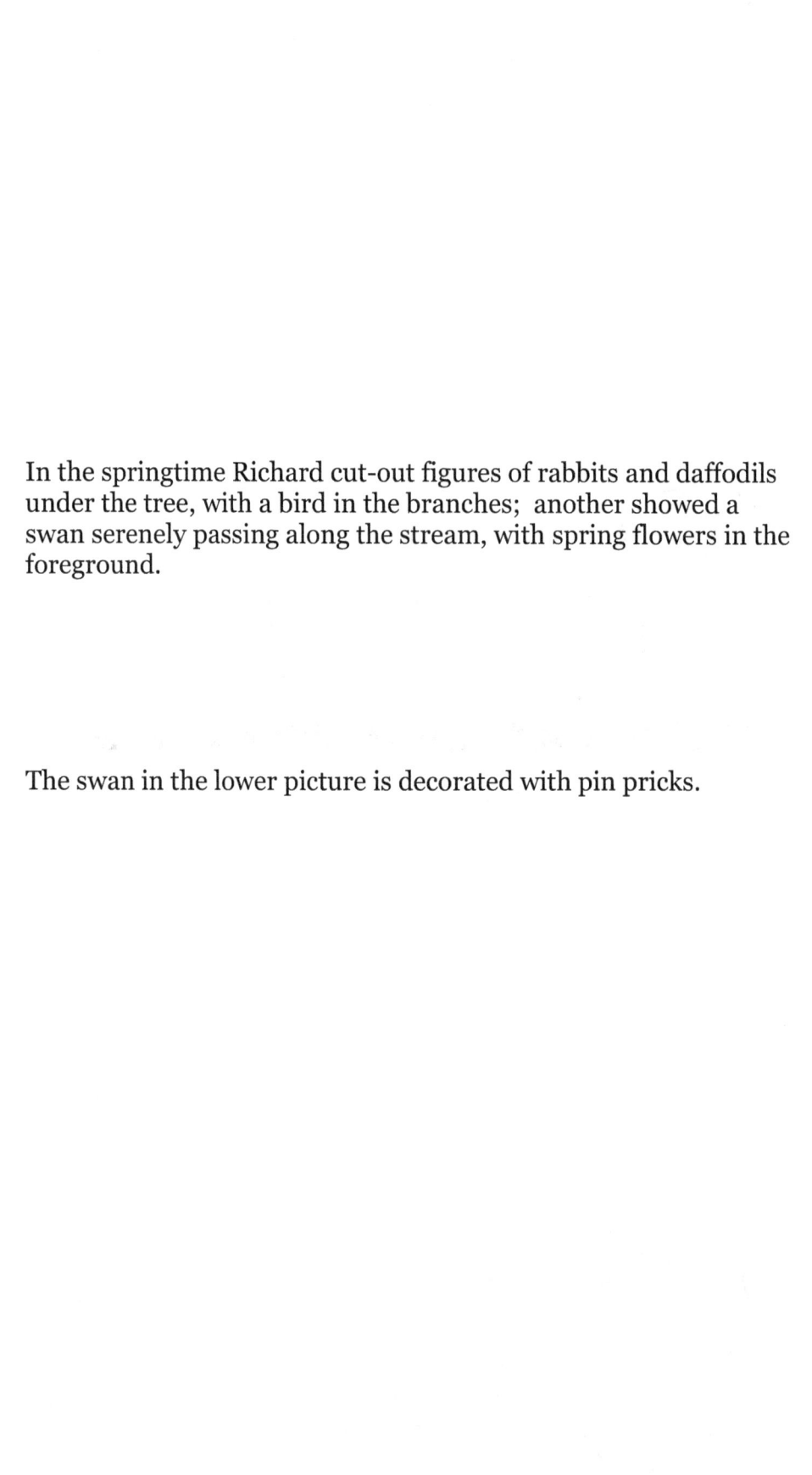

In the springtime Richard cut-out figures of rabbits and daffodils under the tree, with a bird in the branches; another showed a swan serenely passing along the stream, with spring flowers in the foreground.

The swan in the lower picture is decorated with pin pricks.

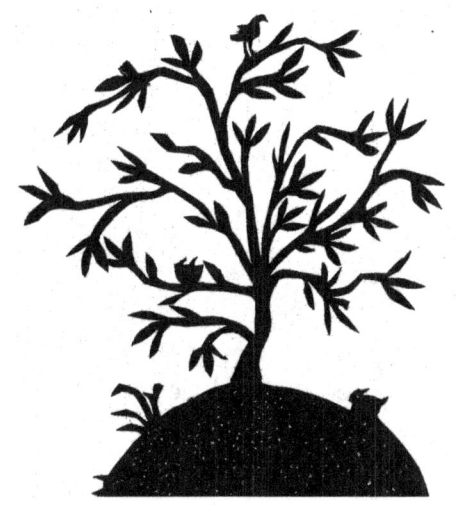

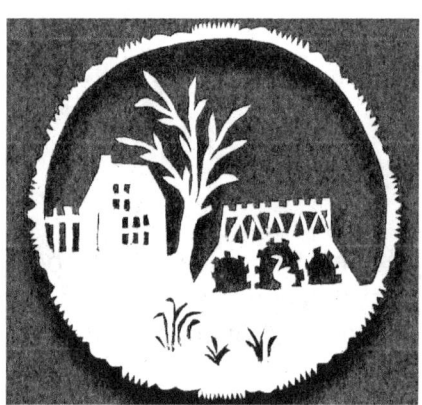

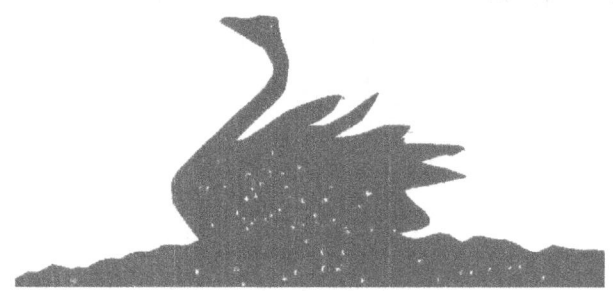

Summertime meant an opportunity to go sight-seeing. In the top picture a coach and horses have just crossed over a bridge. People are relaxing on a boat and a swan sails serenely by....

Richard would also go down to the banks of the River Windrush at Bourton-on-the-Water and cut reeds. These would be stripped down to the white pithy centre, dried in the sun, and then dipped in animal fat or oil to make rushlight candles.

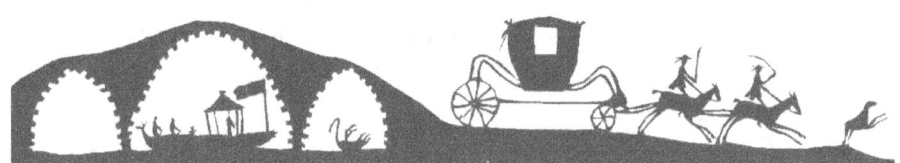
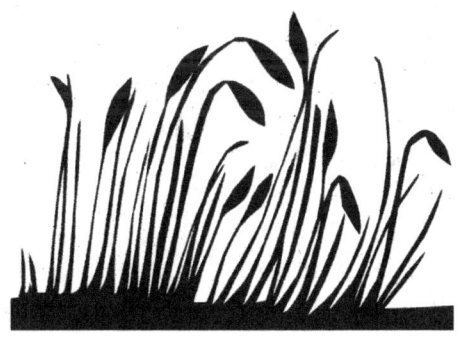

Some of the cut-outs show the fashion for chinoiserie in the second half of the Eighteenth Century. Just about everything could be adorned with the willow pattern, as in this decorated plate:

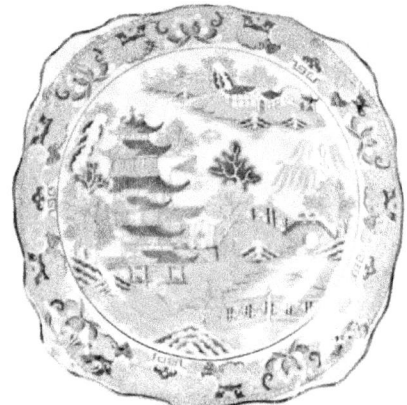 These designs clearly influenced Richard. Here he shows a lady reading in a Chinese style temple, while a young couple walk by hand-in-hand. The tree is shown in the Chinese style.

The lower picture shows an interesting mix of Richard's favourite motifs – the deer chewing the grass, the fawn being suckled, and the Chinese temple and bridge.

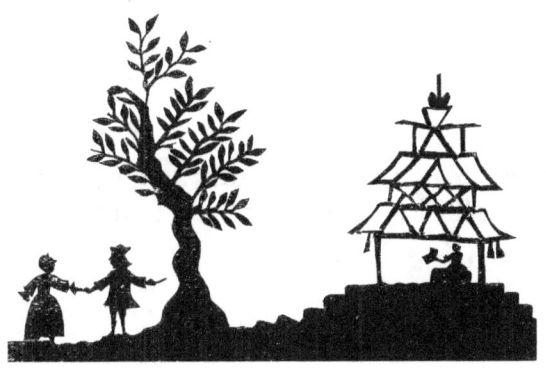

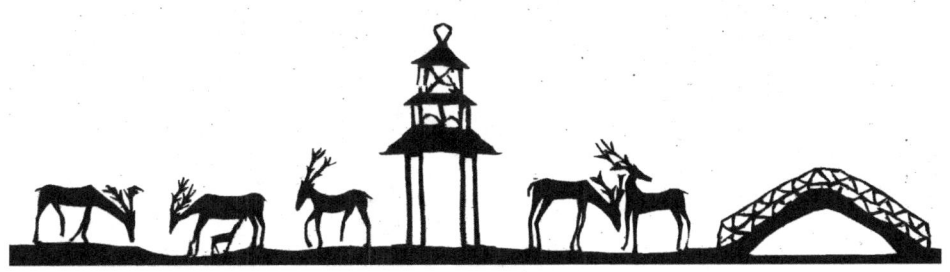

Another Anglo-Chinese scene, with Richard showing his oriental temple on the left of what is otherwise a quintessentially English rural view.

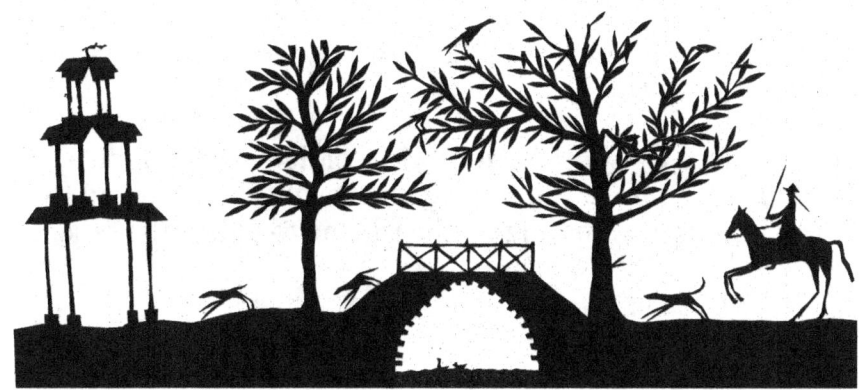

Richard did a series of paper cut-outs showing both naval ships and merchantmen.

In the top picture a shore battery with soldiers and cannon appear to be standing guard. A ship flying an ensign is moored and two men can be seen clambering up the rigging to adjust the sails.

In the lower picture three ships are under sail (with their penants streaming out in front of them) and the front vessel appears to be coming out of the water. Hardly visible in this print is the scallop-shaped cuts which Richard has made, to create the impression of waves in the foreground. It is fairly clear from this that Richard was no sailor - these are representations of sailing ships, not necessarily accurate!

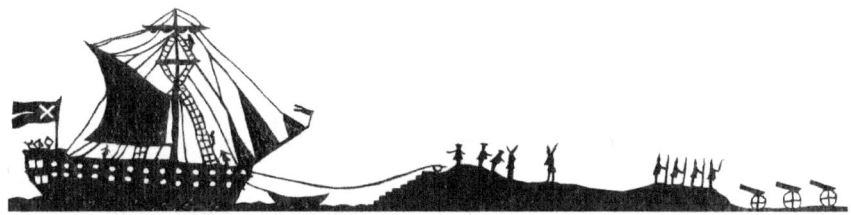

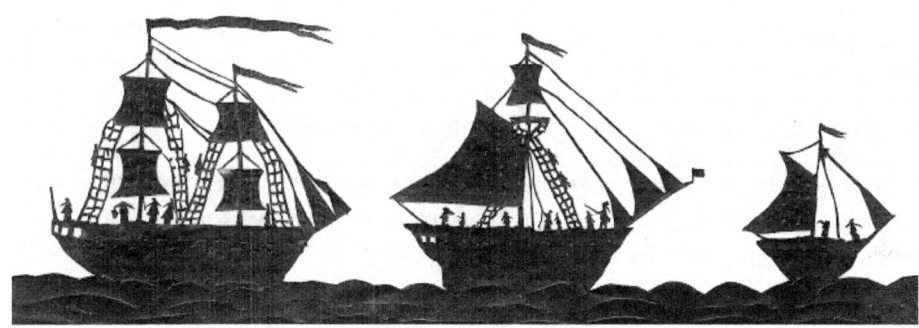

Scenes of commercial activity are also shown. In the top picture men row out to a ship riding the waves further out in the harbour. Soldiers stand guard on the shore – and incidentally they were originally upright but two of them have ended up leaning forward at a crazy angle, thanks to being folded that way for two centuries....

In the lower picture a crane prepares to load or unload cargo brought to the shore. There is no attempt to show scale or perspective.

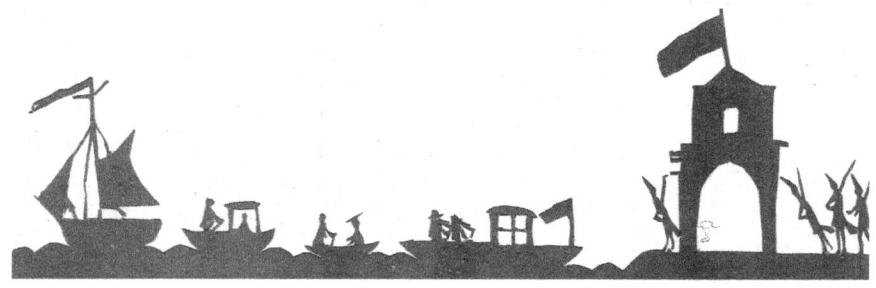

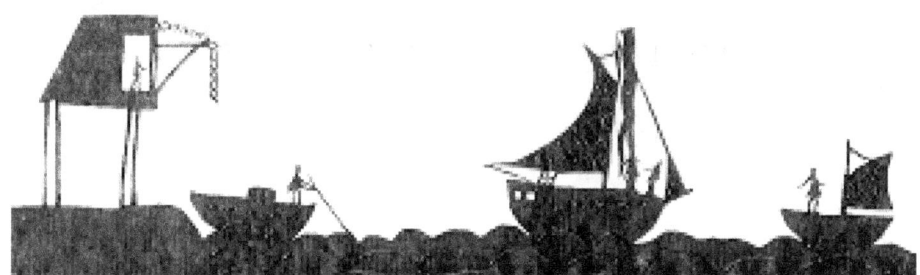

Sometimes Richard cut out scenes which appear to connect up. In the upper picture there seems to be a sort of procession – soldiers escort a carriage topped by a ducal coronet; in front of the four horsemen a group of four people are marching off the page....

... and seem to re-appear in the lower picture, marching in single-file.

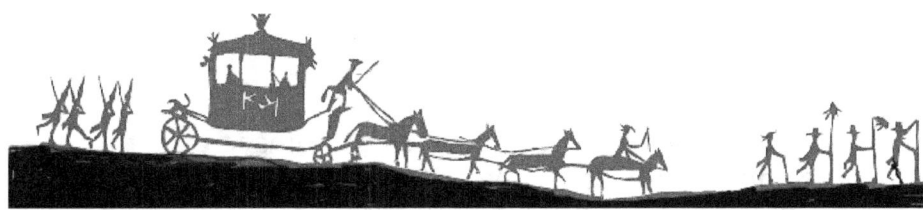

The detail on some of the cut-outs is extraordinary, as in this rapier (compare with a real one shown below). The cut-out is five inches long.

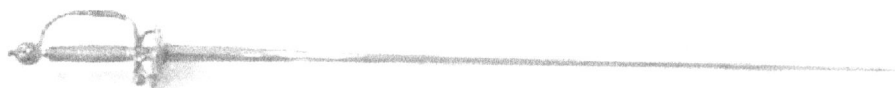

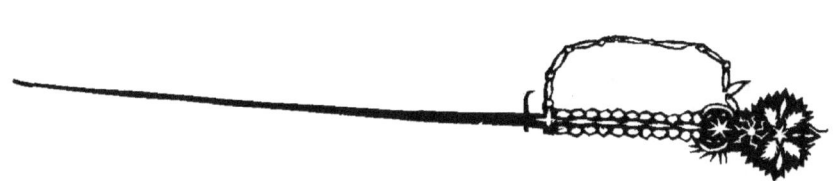

Richard often showed cavalry – here, going at a lively pace:

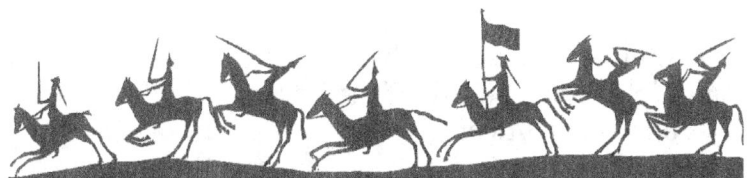

These two are interesting because they are nearly identical. Both show six horses in a row. The gait of the horses in both illustrations is almost identical save for the pair on the extreme right which have been transposed. This suggests that Richard either did the scene so often he could do it from memory, or, more likely, that he first drew a template using pencil and paper, and then copied it using scissors. For some reason he allowed 'artistic licence' to transpose the gait on two of the horses.

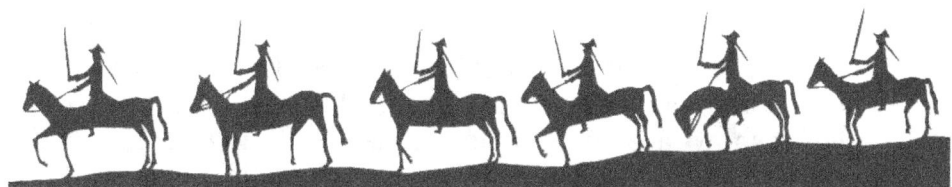

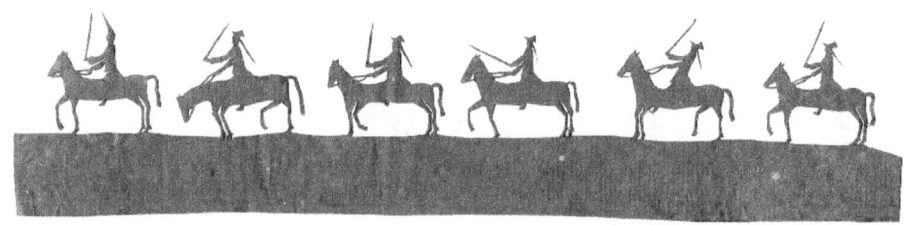

The finest of all the cut-outs was this memorial made by Richard in 1780 to commemorate the death of his beloved first wife, Eleanor. It shows a Chinese-style temple containing a coffin, and Richard has hand-written 'In Memoriam E Hall', her age in Latin ('Aet.46') and her date of death ('Obit 11th January 1780'). On the back, minute writing repeats her name.
The original is barely more than an inch across, and it is shown in both black and white versions to emphasise the delicacy of the cutting. The full delicacy is shown in the magnified version - just imagine putting in that amount of detail into a piece of paper hardly bigger than a watch face!

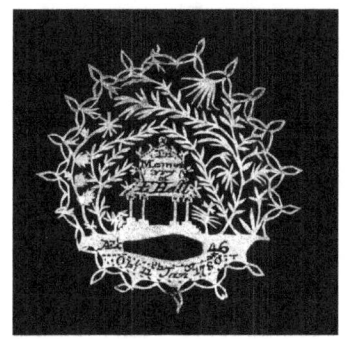
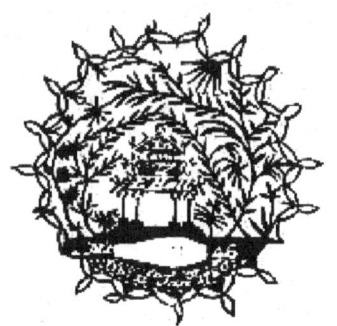
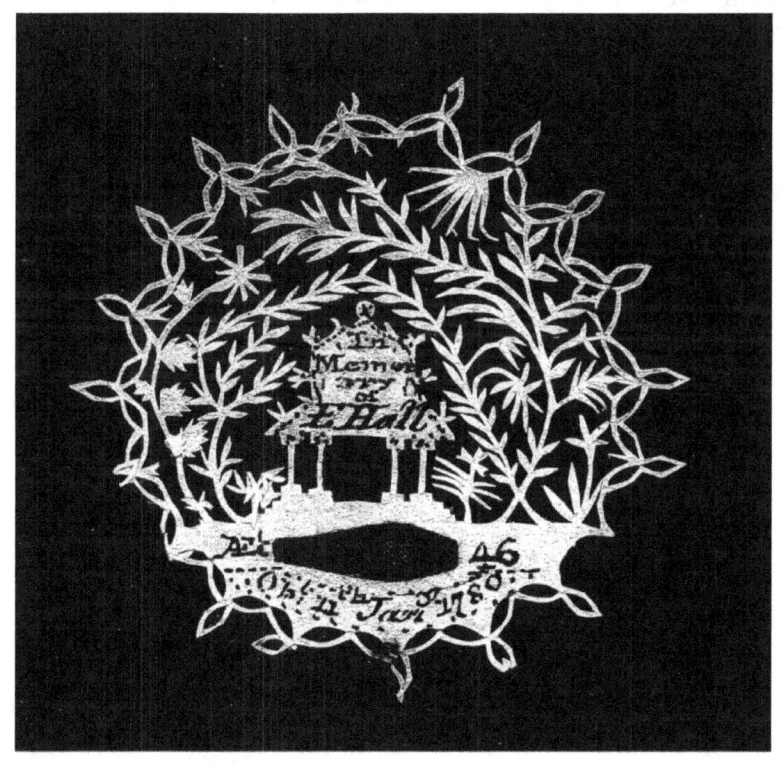

Finally a few miscellaneous cut-outs – a sprig of lily-of the-valley, a roundel showing a figure holding an anchor dated 1798, and a curious picture of goodness-knows-what! It appears to represent a giant angel blowing a trumpet from the rooftop, above a room in which a lady is taking tea; a man emerges from a building opposite carrying what appears to be a watering can, while a dog scampers ahead....

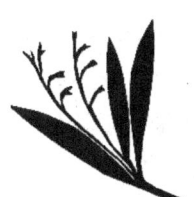

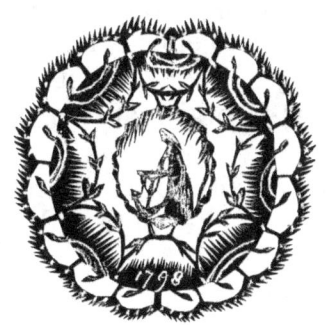

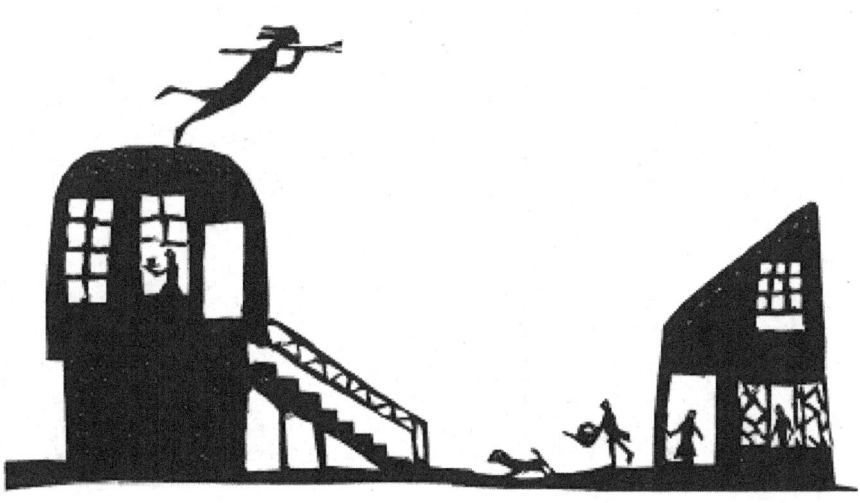

About the author

Mike Rendell retired from the legal profession in 2003 and divides his time between the Costa Blanca in Spain and a home in the U.K. on the edge of Dartmoor.

In addition to writing *The Journal of a Georgian Gentleman* (which is in effect Richard Hall's biography wrapped up as a social history of the 18th Century) Mike writes a regular blog on all-things-Georgian at **http://blog.mikerendell.com**

More details appear at his website at **http://mikerendell.com** and he can be contacted at **info@mikerendell.com**

www.ingramcontent.com/pod-product-compliance
Lightning Source LLC
Chambersburg PA
CBHW081243180526
45171CB00005B/526